T0394941

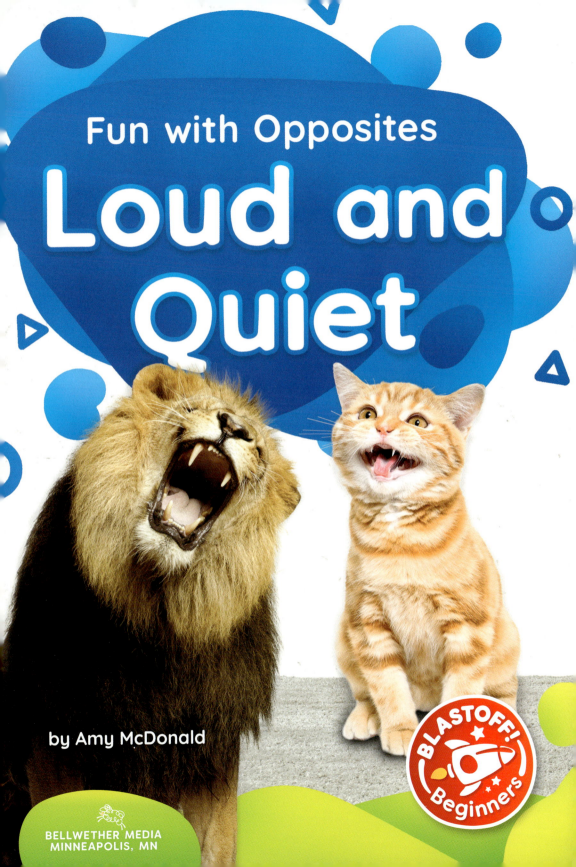

Blastoff! Beginners are developed by literacy experts and educators to meet the needs of early readers. These engaging informational texts support young children as they begin reading about their world. Through simple language and high frequency words paired with crisp, colorful photos, Blastoff! Beginners launch young readers into the universe of independent reading.

Sight Words in This Book

a	he	little	then	your
and	is	of	this	
are	it	the	we	

This edition first published in 2026 by Bellwether Media, Inc.

No part of this publication may be reproduced in whole or in part without written permission of the publisher. For information regarding permission, write to Bellwether Media, Inc., Attention: Permissions Department, 3500 American Blvd W, Suite 150, Bloomington, MN 55431.

Library of Congress Cataloging-in-Publication Data

LC record for Loud and Quiet available at: https://lccn.loc.gov/2025003235

Text copyright © 2026 by Bellwether Media, Inc. BLASTOFF! BEGINNERS and associated logos are trademarks and/or registered trademarks of Bellwether Media, Inc. Bellwether Media is a division of FlutterBee Education Group.

Editor: Rebecca Sabelko   Designer: Laura Sowers

Printed in the United States of America, North Mankato, MN.

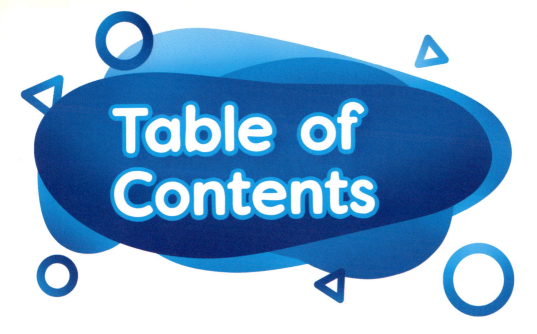

Table of Contents

Surprise Party!	4
Two Opposites	6
Loud and Quiet Things	12
Loud and Quiet Facts	22
Glossary	23
To Learn More	24
Index	24

Surprise Party!

We stayed quiet. Then we loudly yelled surprise!

Two Opposites

Loud and quiet are **volumes**.

Loud means a lot of **sound**.

Quiet means
a little sound.
Shhh.

Loud and Quiet Things

A roaring lion is loud.
A **purring** cat is quiet.

Playgrounds are noisy! Libraries are quiet.

library

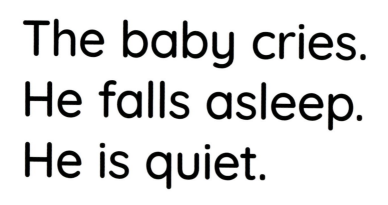

The baby cries.
He falls asleep.
He is quiet.

The airplane is loud.
This bird flies quietly.

airplane

Think of your favorite game. Is it loud or quiet?

Loud and Quiet Facts

Loud and Quiet Around Us

playing loudly

reading quietly

Something Loud and Quiet

airplane

bird

Glossary

purring

making a soft sound

sound

noise

volumes

amounts of sound

To Learn More

ON THE WEB

FACTSURFER

Factsurfer.com gives you a safe, fun way to find more information.

1. Go to www.factsurfer.com.

2. Enter "loud and quiet" into the search box and click 🔍.

3. Select your book cover to see a list of related content.

Index

airplane, 18
asleep, 16
baby, 16
bird, 18
cat, 12
cries, 16
game, 20
libraries, 14
lion, 12
playgrounds, 14
sound, 8, 10
surprise, 4
volumes, 6

The images in this book are reproduced through the courtesy of: Eric Isselee, front cover, p. 12; Sonsedska Yuliia, front cover; stockphoto-graf, p. 3; Ladanifer, pp. 4-5; AnnaStills, pp. 6-7; Bobcat_art, p. 8; Krtek1, pp. 8-9; GOLFX, pp. 10, 22 (top reading); LightField Studios, pp. 10-11; StockPhotoPro, pp. 12-13; BearFotos, p. 14; Anant Jadhav, pp. 14-15; Jjustas, p. 16; Monkey Business, pp. 16-17; Caftor, p. 18; Jo, pp. 18-19; Southworks, pp. 20-21; jayzynism, p. 22 (top playground); New Africa, p. 22 (top soccer); Synthetic Messiah, p. 22 (airplane); Sari ONeal, p. 22 (bird); HannahMarieCecilia, p. 23 (purring); SteffenTravel, p. 23 (sound); THANYAKRIS, p. 23 (volumes).